Memory of Mosaic Moments

Memory of Mosaic Moments

Poems by

John Lawrence Darretta

© 2026 John Lawrence Darretta. All rights reserved.
This material may not be reproduced in any form, published,
reprinted, recorded, performed, broadcast,
rewritten or redistributed without
the explicit permission of John Lawrence Darretta.
All such actions are strictly prohibited by law.

Cover design by Shay Culligan
Cover image by Havva Yılmaz on Unsplash
Vector illustration by Ritam Baishya on Unsplash

ISBN: 979-8-90146-802-9
Library of Congress Control Number: 2026932860

Kelsay Books
502 South 1040 East, A-119
American Fork, Utah 84003
Kelsaybooks.com

for all my former students

Acknowledgments

I am grateful to my dear family, friends, and students who read my poems throughout the years and offered their comments and suggestions that always made me rethink, revise and move on. I would like to thank Alexandra Paige and Steven Grubiak for their reading, correcting, and commenting on my manuscript.

Sincere acknowledgment is given to the publications and online venues in which the following poems (some in earlier versions) first appeared:

Best Poets of 2024 (Eber & Wein, 2025): "Fluff and Tatters"

The Cape Cod Times: "A Wake in April 1968," "On the Trail with Granny"

The Cornelian: "Next Stop, Please"

The Fioretti: "Dionysian Disco"

Here and Now, There and Then (Kelsay Books, 2024): "Fluff and Tatters,"

Nature's Wheel (Kelsay Books, 2019): "Gallivant"

Poetry.com: "Political Ring"

Quilted Thoughts (Eber & Wein Publishing, 2024*)*: "Gallivant"

Many thanks to Karen Kelsay and the staff of Kelsay Books for their pleasant and efficient assistance throughout the editing and publication of *Memory of Mosaic Moments*.

Contents

Nature Speaks	15
Next Stop, Please!	16
While Waiting for the Mountains to Fall	17
Lessons of Life	18
Time Passes	20
Waiting	21
Listen	22
A Buddhist Tale	23
You	24
The Empty Table	25
Gallivant	26
Hello	27
Greetings	28
Angelic Phone	29
Leda's Lament	30
Dionysian Disco	32
Gibson's Girl	33
Parasols in the Rain	34
Fluff and Tatters	36
On the Trail with Granny	37
Political Ring	38
Morning Light	39
Watching Waters	40
In the Beginning	41
Iris	42
The Rabbit and the Hawk	43
Haiku	44
Seed	46
A Loss	48
A Life	49
A Wake in April, 1968	50

Love is . . .	51
Eternal Rewards	52
Earth, Sea and Sky	53

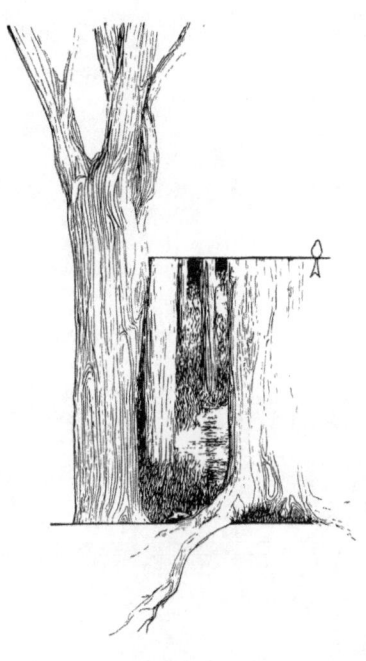

Nature Speaks

A rustling in the wind
A rippling in the brook
A tapping on lush leaves
A trilling of a bird
A buzzing of a bee

The bleating of a lamb
The clicking of a whale
The crying in a crib
The lapping in the sea
The swishing of the sand

A brewing storm in the sky
A dripping on windowsills
A crinkling of winter hail
A crackling fire on the hills
A whistling wind through the trees

Listen, nature speaks

Next Stop, Please!

I have boarded many trains
and watched steam spurt up
on windows—spread and roll.

I have seen foolish people
depress on cool glass,
breathing out warm vapors
like martyrs—brave and bold.

I loathe railroad saints;
they are cold and vague.
Knock them on the floor,
they smash—trash and ash.

I love common saints;
they are warm and real.
And knocking them down,
they bounce up—blood and flesh.

If I wanted to look at bland faces,
I would always ride
on grey subway's miles,
but I will not—for I have spent my life
longing for golden smiles.

While Waiting for the Mountains to Fall

When I was young
I was never told

it is the lover
who loves someone
yet not everyone

it is the believer
who believes
but who also has some doubts

it is the philosopher
who knows about life
yet not always how to live

it is the artist
who sees through things
but is often blind to the world

it is the poet
who says it with bright words
but fractures it in the heart

no one ever told me
but now I know.

Lessons of Life

I went to local schools with many tots and teens
       so pushed and pulled
       sweet soapy smelled
       scholastically interred
I never learned.

I have been to mobbed malls with plenty of shoppers
       escalatored
       bargain battered
       serviceably perturbed
I would not buy.

I have been to ball parks with bleachers full of fans
       gum wrap rollers
       hotdog holders
       diamondly disturbed
I could not play.

I have been in Times Square with mobs of revelers
       smoking lookers
       back-slap slappers
       unpleasantly absurd
I did not join.

Only now, by myself,
Now and here all alone
do I discern
to be more positive
about community

and learn to live
        pressed on forward
        elevated upward
        running over and stirred.

Time Passes

Nanosecond: One billionth part of a second
Microsecond: One millionth part of a second
Millisecond: One thousandth part of a second
Centisecond: One hundredth part of a second

Second: One sixtieth part of a minute
Minute: 60 seconds
Hour: 60 minutes
Day: 24 hours
Week: 7 days (Sun., Mon., Tues., Wed., Thurs., Fri., Sat.)
Month: 4 weeks
Year: 12 months (Jan., Feb., Mar., Apr., May, Jun., Jul., Aug., Sep., Oct., Nov., Dec.)

Decade: 10 years
Century: 100 years
Millennium: 1,000 years
Era: Millions of years (periods of history, subdivision of eons)
Eon: billions of years

Time passes to eternity

Waiting

I am always waiting.
>Waiting in a restaurant craving to eat
>Waiting in my room for the rising heat
>Waiting in my doctor's office hoping to be well
>Waiting in the church for ringing of the bell
>Waiting on a bank line to cash my check
>Waiting on a ship for a sunlit deck
>Waiting at the bus stop to get where I'm going
>Waiting at school for the gift of knowing
>Waiting at theater longing for the show to begin

I'll be at the Gate of Heaven, waiting to get in.

Listen

Listen not with your ears alone but with your heart,
    not just outer noises but inner whispers, too.
Heed not external cautions only but internal calls,
    attending to what you see, hear, and what you feel.

Listen to the sounds of nature, the colors of art,
    and to the passion of love and the joy of spirit.
Embrace new feelings available to each and all,
    with awareness enabling us, as we listen to life.

Listen for the most beautiful of all,
    the meeting and greeting of your true self.

A Buddhist Tale

A little salt doll that lived on earth came upon
a powerful body of matter it had never seen before.
It was blue, deep, grand and moved in undulating waves.

The salt doll slowly approached
the wavering waters and said,
    "What are you?"
A wonderful sound echoed from the sea,
    "Touch me."
The salt doll approached it,
    and dipped a toe into the moving mass.

It pulled back to find its toe was gone.
In amazement, it asked again,
    "Who are you?"
The voice from the sea replied once more,
    "Touch me."
The salt doll put its arms into the swirling surf
    and soon they have vanished.
It asked more emphatically.
    "Who are you?"
The beckoning waters said continuously.
    "Touch me,"
Intrigued, the salt doll walked into the sea solemnly repeating,
    "Who are you?"
    and it began to slowly disappear.

As the salt doll dissolved into the deep sea,
the mighty waters affectionately answered
in a sweet and soothing sound,

    "I am you. You are me."

You

I don't care if you're male or female;
If your skin is dark brown or light white,
If your eyes are green or blue,
If your hair is gray or blonde,
If you're short or tall, portly or thin.

They're parts of your physical identity;
It's not *What* you are that finally matters,
It's *Who* you are that really matters.
Whatever communal coop you're in,
What's the utmost important is *Who* you are.

So, *What* does *Who* bring to you:
Love or Hate, Good or Evil,
Or petty Indifference?
You are gifted with free will,
And things that are important
Are the choices that make you
        You.

The Empty Table

Seated at mother's table
to enjoy her Italian meal
were anyone and everyone
European or American
African and Asian
Polish or Irish
Christian and Jewish
Male or female
Healthy and frail
Gay or Straight
Thin and overweight
Short or tall.

One in all.

Now mother's gone
The food is done
Years have passed on
The table is worn
No longer all in one
Each a political pawn
Used for *what* they are
Not loved for *who* they are.

What happened?

No longer a meal of splendor
Only a political agenda.

Gallivant

Away the world with willow wands
scatter leaves for Sybils
and if you will let vagabonds
run down from Wiltshire hills.

But never go where rainbows end
and dancers capriole
for footfalls follow freely there
in sordid rigmarole.

Or walk the way of Willibrord
and cross the Isle of Man
fill all the world with willow wands
and leaves from sacred hands.

Hello

Hello. Hello!

The world is gnarled with stuttering static
       and galling vibrations.
The world is muddled with missed messages
       that no one will receive.

You call and drop before I can pick up.
       I answer again and noisy clatter calls.
I call and deflated silence answers.
       You finally answer and your speech is scrawled.
You call again but cannot leave a message.

Who can unscramble static and stutter?
Who can rephrase vacuous vibration?
Who can accept silence and rejection?

Please let me know.
       Leave a message.

Hello. Hello! Hell . . .

Greetings

Hello, Goodbye
is all we ever hear

Hello, Goodbye
we lose the meaning
we never find the words

Before we know
the hello dies its death
in the birth
of another goodbye

Angelic Phone

The celestial host is a hotspot, and it's free.
With my quick connection I can reach all my friends
      across the land or across the sea.
My images and thoughts fly airways.
      My wishes climb up on mountains.
      My complaints cross over plains.
It's so beautiful, and so easy to care for and handle,
      and it evokes the curiosities of life.
Why does the physical always try to copy the metaphysical?
Why would I ever give up my perfect sacred subscription?

Leda's Lament

Animate sea-glass eyes
sirocco-flesh boy
with lavender-oil fingertips
sprouting violet where tides give way.
Pomegranate spills through lips
flickering across an umber dream
singing of a blue-green bay
dyed by the morning sun.

Initiate trembling sighs
sea-stained smiles bite bedded swan
streaking mouths with carmine plum.
Heather colored hairs float down
on sea-glass eyes closed to sight
but known to heated lust
slithering over tawny skin
warmed by the flaming sun.

Consummate heated cries
trembling touch of passioned boy
in saffroned hills with perfume balm
of fevered flesh and jolts of quaking limbs.
Too soon the moment passes
and blurring sea-glass eyes are lost
to dreams of fading molt of swan
burnished in the blazing sun.

I wait by the caves of Gortys
watching the sky with clouded eyes
forgetting perfume and pomegranate
remembering old, ruined gods
longing for a boy while crying for a bird.
Under an echo of thundering waves
and a wild rush of squealing gulls
I lift a dying kiss to the setting sun.

Dionysian Disco

With the lavender moon
the erotic zebra
wails a dithyramb
as the writhing satyrs
wave their buttocks
toward the sun.
A lewd Leda
slithers across the floor
crying for a bird
while tight-lipped Sibyls
close their eyes
and sip white wine.
Niobe is stoned
and the gorgons
laugh.

Gibson's Girl

Once, I was Gibson's girl
round cheeked and rosy
placed in high delight
as a lover's ecstasy.

At times blushing or laughing
I primped in communal sight
as youthful charm.
I was the brilliant star.

Then the aging new world
opened so far and wide
exposed me in gossipy mags
as an old and fading light.

Now, I hide behind my screen
fearing snooping gazers
who come to gape at a former beauty
blemished with crepey skin.

Parasols in the Rain

With their umbrellas
splashed with colors
fluttering up and down
like old-world parasols,
the mourning family
hurries toward the church.

8:20 on a drizzling morning,
they stop for a traffic light.

The little boys move
 toward the front in running pace
to keep up with their mother
now that father's gone,
and the older girls walk
straight and beautiful behind.

They will all be together
 in fervent and peaceful prayer
where you can see their love
a pastiche of color all about them,
as if covered and protected by their father
with a vigilant floating canopy.

It is good to watch them
in their warm and dry harmony.

They are no fragile contrast
to the mother and daughter
sleeping off their tiring dates

with matted hair on pillows
streaked with last night's lipstick,
and drowsy dispositions
protected under synthetic sheets,
breathing in the damp, stale air
of some active death.

8:20 on a drizzling morning,
they did not stop for a traffic light.

Fluff and Tatters

Look at the stunning starlet
posed on a golden chair.
Her lips are shiny scarlet,
streaked and fluffed the hair.
Her nails all glazed like fire,
before the curtain rises.

Look at the lady haggard
stooped to a soiled ground.
Her dirty hair is ragged,
iced fingers search around.
A crumb or two, a bone will do,
before the curtain falls.

What do we see as the world moves?
Who can it be that matters?
Is it all for shine and fluff
and not the stains and tatters?

On the Trail with Granny

We're off on our morning run
I'm stirring and on the go
      You're serene and rather slow
I'm sixteen; you're sixty-one
      You're granny; I'm the grandson
I'm all show and you're all know
      yet together we will glow
Moving on our morning run

Political Ring

The circle of Politics is
a flat ring that
curves from the Center
all the way to
Far Right or Far Left.

At the end of the curve
white-hooded klans
black-masked pinkos
meet and merge in
a mean extreme.

What they have in sight
is all the same
except that one sees from
the left eye and
the other the right.

Each side is filled
with hate and anger
desiring to control
longing to rule
the subservient other.

The good notion is
that they represent
no-one and nothing
between themselves and
the rest of the ring.

Morning Light

As time passes on its way
It speaks to us in gold and gray
We get a bright start at dawning
And move through a bustling day
We slow down in the evening
And then move to a closing night
We pass through shadowed darkening
And back to the morning light

Watching Waters

Water moves
> Slow or fast
> Drizzles or downpours
> Flows or Floods
> Fades or Feeds

Water aids and creates
Water calms and comforts
Water cleans and redeems
Water hallows and thrives.
> A wonder of being.

In the Beginning

Everything and anyone that exists must have a creator.
The statue of David would not exist if Michelangelo had
 not created it.
Macbeth would not exist if Shakespeare had not created it.
I Know Why the Caged Bird Sings would not exist if Maya
 Angelou had not created it.
"America the Beautiful" would not exist if Katherine Bates
 and Samuel Ward had not created it.
The Statue of Liberty would not exist if Frederic Auguste
 Bartholdi had not created it.
The White House would not exist if James Hoban had not
 created it.
The mobile phone would not exist if Martin Cooper had not
 created it.
The universe would not exist if God had not created it.

Man and woman would never have existed if God had not
 created them.
Michelangelo's parents would not have existed if their
 parents had not created them.
Michelangelo would not have existed if his parents had not
 created him.

Everything and everyone that exists must have a creator.
If not, the statue of David would never have existed.

Iris

Passion plucked from Elysian Fields
        night squeezed of a darkened life
mauve monsters fused with gold optimism
        on bicolored heads of Rome with Grecian necks
blooming from white perfumed eyes

The Rabbit and the Hawk

A cute, tiny rabbit would hop and feed on the lawn at least
    twice a day.
It was, as usual, alert to its surroundings and timid.
When I quietly walked by and talked soothingly,
    telling it that it was adorable, and I had no intention
    of harming it, the rabbit would not run away.
It would look at me, tilt its head and continue to eat.
I looked forward to the rabbit on the lawn as I passed each day
    on my trip to feed fish at the pond.
Yesterday, it was dead on a rock along the edge of the water.
It looked flawless; yet, when I took it to bury,
    I saw an awful indent on its back.
Evidently a hawk had taken it and dropped it from above.
I could not blame the bird, as this was the way of nature,
    and I often looked above to admire its graceful flight.
But there is now a grave in the garden, and the friend that I long
    for is gone from the lawn.
  Something is gone from the lawn and I long for it.

Haiku

fading orange rose
bright glistening burning sun
changing everything

balmy evening breeze
wavering rainbow sunlight
a peacock's full fan

peacocks, wrens, and swans
each one a different note
with the selfsame song

Winter cardinals
On white frosty slabs of snow
Like blood drops on sheets

Hot, cold, wet or dry
All things have an opposite
Light, dark, good or bad

Seed

A small seed falls from a bending stem of wheat.
Carried by an arc of wind to a small nesting place in the
    soil,
it waits in darkness to be nurtured in the earth.

Advanced with moisture, stirred by light, it begins to peek
    above the ground,
growing taller and larger amidst the trials of its growth,
    heat by day, cold by night,
falling drops from sun showers, driving rain, breeze or
    blast. It bears it all.
Reaching its potential, it is found pleasing and soon
    harvested.
Then, from the indolence of storage, to winnowing buffets
    through grinding crucible,
it changes into flour.

In its new life, the flour is sifted, mixed with bits of sugar,
    salt and butter
Warm water laced with yeast is added; then, it is left to rise
    as batter,
but only to be pulled and kneaded and shaped into a new
    form,
placed in a confining pan and left alone again, until it is
    warmed
and baked into an even newer self: a crusty, soft self,
with a heated aroma that is second to none.

But its transformation as bread does not stop there; for it
 was made to be torn apart again,
to please and nourish another member of nature. So, you
 eat the delicious bread,
you savor it and it fills you and it begins to become
 something new.
The seed has not died; it has not ceased from existence; it
 continues.

A Loss

Winter came and autumn died
husbands and brothers next door
I saw their last I-love-you
reverberate in a sighing wind.

In the wail of a dirge
dry leaves trembled and fell
as the crying birds flew off
and she told them to hurry back.

Her saddened steps echoing
on the hard crust of the earth
where underneath all things
lay listening-waiting.

She was cold and pale with tears
and wept to the setting sun—
"Comfort him in the soft warmth
of your calm and golden smile."

A Life

Like the night
        transitions into dawn
Birth rises to Life
        intensely growing
Life descends to Death
        dust falling to dusk
Like the dove
        it flies to Eternity

A Wake in April, 1968

I was leaving campus, heading downtown
      to buy lilies for Easter.

You asked me to walk with you across the field
to a professor's house, about a philosophy exam,
      as I recall.

A philosophy exam, you were quite worried.
I smiled and said, in my sure but careless way,
      "There's nothing to fear in philosophies."

Then mindfully we stepped, side by side,
and walked across the field. You were concerned,
      I was convinced.

Halls of Ivy are done, and you are gone.
Now here I stand, and over there you rest,
      Laid out among the lilies.

Crossing a rice field, far from the town, so I am told.
What was on your mind and what did it behold?
      Were you worried, with no one there beside you?

I should have walked with you between the mines,
sighed and said, in a sure and careful way,
      "There's something to fear in philosophies."

Love is . . .

Love is a rose.
No, not a rose,
but almost a rose,
with sharp prickling thorns
and dry pollen dust
on blood-dropped petals.
Yet, blossoming
Into bouquets.

Eternal Rewards

In the world of opposites,
one has the free will to choose,
between our youth and old age
from birth to death.

Amidst failure and success
      poorness and wealth.

Through pleasure and displeasure
      illness and health.

With lies or truth
      doubts or firm faith.

It is our inclination,
positive or negative,
to choose toward good or evil
God or Devil

leading us to
rewards of Eternity:

      Heaven or Hell.

Earth, Sea and Sky

The Earth's surface upholds and nourishes me
    Here and now
The Sea's water stimulates and soothes me
    Here and now
The Sky's air invigorates and inspires me
    Here and now
They teach me and lead me to the eternal
    Here and now

About the Author

A former metropolitan New York college professor, John Darretta now lives on Cape Cod. John holds a Ph.D. in English from Fordham University and has authored books and articles on American literature and Italian cinema. As Fulbright Professor to Italy, he taught at universities in Milan and Turin, where he studied Italian film at Museo Nazionale del Cinema.

A specialist on Italian films of the neorealist period, his *Vittorio De Sica* (G. K. Hall) was the first full-length work in English on the films of the noted director. He is also author of *Before the Sun Has Set: Retribution in the Fiction of Flannery O'Connor* (Peter Lang Publishing). He recently authored *Sacred Senses in Sacred Space: A Journey into a Church* (Gatekeeper Press).

For John, writing poetry has been a passion since high school days. His creative work has appeared in *America Magazine, Penwood Review, Avalon Literary Review, Pilgrim Journal, Haiku Journal, First Literary Review-East,* and other venues. Collections of his poems have been published in *Nature's Wheel* (Kelsay Books, 2019) and *Here and Now, There and Then* (Kelsay Books, 2024).

www.ingramcontent.com/pod-product-compliance
Lightning Source LLC
Chambersburg PA
CBHW031639160426
43196CB00006B/482